PROVEN TIPS FOR SUCCESS
FROM RECENT GRADS WHO KILLED IT

Michael Seringhaus & Brian Savage

He-Dog Press, 2017

Revised & Updated Second Edition

© 2014, 2017 by Michael Seringhaus & Brian Savage.
This edition © 2017.
Original e-book edition © 2014.

Printed in the United States of America. All rights reserved. No part of this book may be reproduced in any manner whatsoever without written permission.

Cover design by Duane Busby.

ISBN: 978-0-9990589-0-9

Published by He-Dog Press, Menlo Park, CA.
www.he-dog.com

Praise for Law School Done Right

"Students who do well in the crucial first year of law school often have the advantage of being clued in early—by a sibling or friend who has already been there—about the strange demands that law school imposes. This little book helps even the odds."

Henry Hansmann
Oscar M. Ruebhausen Professor of Law
Yale Law School

"In light of the high cost of law school and transformational changes affecting the legal profession, prospective and current law students need all the guidance they can get. You have just one chance to do law school, so do it right – with the help of this wonderfully concise, highly readable resource."

David Lat
Managing Editor, *Above the Law*
Author, *Supreme Ambitions: A Novel*

"Legal education's peculiar culture and process are often overlooked by those beginning their pursuit of the JD. Seringhaus and Savage offer law students a set of immensely helpful questions to ask, combined with nuggets of sage advice for navigating law school."

Christopher L. Griffin, Jr.
Assistant Professor of Law
William & Mary Law School

Why This Book?

Law school really is like nothing else. As recent grads, we often found ourselves sharing advice with friends who were just starting out. After a while, we decided to create a guide containing the very best tips for law school success.

We asked ourselves one simple question: **What do we wish we'd known when we started law school?** We compiled our top tips, then turned to our network. We polled a couple dozen of our colleagues and former classmates, all recent graduates, and asked them to review our tips and contribute their own. Our group included grads of schools both inside and outside the U.S. News Top 50; grads who landed judicial clerkships (including U.S. Supreme, Federal Appellate, Federal District, and State Supreme courts), as well as associates at top national law firms, in-house counsel, and even young law professors. These folks did it right.

Then, we cut and pared and distilled down to just the best advice. And the result is this trim little book. **No filler, just the tips.** Because whether you're already in law school, or just thinking about going, you've got enough to read.

We hope that you love *Law School Done Right*, that you refer to it often, and that it helps you make the most of your time at law school.

—Michael Seringhaus & Brian Savage
Menlo Park, CA

Contents

Before We Begin 9
Choosing a Law School 13
The Old-Fashioned Social Network 25
Rankings & Grades 33
Class Time 39
Exam Time 51
Choosing Courses 65
Aiming High 75
Applications & Interviews 87
Other Stuff 95

Concluding Words 105
About the Authors 106

1

Before We Begin

Is law school right for you?

BEFORE WE BEGIN

Be sure, to the extent you can.

Law school is expensive and time-consuming. People often say, "you can do anything with a law degree." You can also do anything *without* a law degree (except be a lawyer).

Particularly if you'll be taking on significant debt to attend, think carefully about whether law school will further your career goals—do you actually want to be a lawyer? Talk to some lawyers and see.

Choosing a Law School

Where to go, where to go?

Choose the best school you can get into.

It's basic advice, but there's a reason we put it first.

If you get into a top law school but are debating attending a considerably lower-ranked one—either for scholarship money, because of geographic preference, or because you think you'll be the big fish in a small pond—don't do it.

Sure, these are reasonable ideas, and in any other profession they might make sense. But lawyers, as a group, are amazingly focused on school prestige. Merit matters, yes, but your law school does too. A lot.

It sounds silly, and it is. But if you take one thing from this book, let it be this: Ignore overall law school rankings at your peril.

Outside the top few, law schools are surprisingly regional.

All else being equal, choose a law school someplace you wouldn't mind working.

The top big-name law schools are considered "national," which basically means that once you graduate, you can work anywhere in the country.

But this effect drops off surprisingly quickly, even within the so-called "top 14" schools. Don't be one of the students—and every year there are many—who attend a solid law school serving a smaller regional market, only to find it's extremely challenging to find work elsewhere.

For admissions purposes, your Ph.D. is an extracurricular.

Law school admissions committees typically rank applicants based on their LSAT scores and undergraduate grades, and only then do they consider other "soft factors."

This is particularly hard to accept when you've just finished graduate school and undergrad is a distant memory. Sad but true: Admissions officers seem to rank a Ph.D. somewhere alongside playing the piano. You'll need to look back to undergrad and hope you delivered the goods.

Beware specialized rankings.

It's become popular for the ranking magazines to rank various legal specialties, and to publish lists of the top law schools for environmental law, intellectual property law, and so on.

As sensible as this may seem, these rankings are a red herring. Pretty much no one in the business pays attention to them. So, to the extent they conflict with the overall rankings, ignore them.

On a broader note, don't worry about choosing a school that offers a strong curriculum in some legal specialty of interest to you. Even if you do end up working in that field—and you may not!—those classes are far less important than you might think.

Beware the scholarship bait-and-switch.

There are some shady law schools out there. Look carefully at any school that offers you a hefty scholarship contingent on maintaining a mid-level GPA. Talk to current and past students before you sign on.

Why? Because schools can do this, and then grade so aggressively that pretty much every student falls below their GPA threshold. Then you lose your scholarship and you're stuck paying full tuition at a second-choice school—and as an added bonus, your deflated grades are too low to transfer out.

Investigate each school's employment and bar passage statistics.

This information is publicly accessible. Don't brush it off as irrelevant: You're spending a lot of money on this degree, and this is one way to research what you're buying.

Employment stats can be gamed. (We've heard stories of law schools hiring unemployed grads for a day to man a reunion welcome table, then chalking them up as "employed" in the annual survey.)

Bar passage rates are harder to tweak.

If your LSAT or grades are weak, consider whether it's worth attending law school.

It's understandably exciting to get into a law school. But if you actually attend a low-tier school, the unfortunate reality is that, at least in the crucial first years, the best legal jobs may simply be closed off to you. For instance, many major law firms simply will not interview candidates from certain lower-ranked schools—even those at the very top of the class.

This may not matter if your family runs a law firm and you have a guaranteed job, but if not, think hard about whether it's worth spending hundreds of thousands of dollars to attend a low-tier school. Try talking to some recent graduates for perspective.

Rankings are a broad brush.

For all our emphasis on rankings here, remember that they're (i) a fairly coarse measure, (ii) based on sometimes silly metrics (think: number of library volumes per full-time student), and (iii) likely to shuffle somewhat year-to-year.

So, while choosing the #9 ranked school over #75 probably makes sense, choosing #9 over #10 may not.

Transferring isn't as easy as it seems.

Don't automatically assume you can enroll in a lower-ranked school, make the dean's list, and transfer to Harvard for 2L.

It happens, but it's rare. Competition can be fierce in first year, and it's almost always easier just to get in where you want to go in the first place.

The Old-Fashioned Social Network

Congrats! You're in law school. Now for the first surprise: It's not all books and exams. The social stuff matters.

Law school is a lot like middle school.

You have a locker. You lug heavy textbooks around in your backpack. You have a full day of classes, mostly with the same people. You may even have a "homeroom." You study. You have exams.

Oh, and people gossip—in a major way.

Make friends with a 3L or recent graduate of your school. Buy them a drink and ask for a candid rundown of courses and professors.

Get tips specific to your school. It's amazing how much institutional knowledge accumulates over just three years.

When you graduate, pay it forward to an incoming student.

Be nice to your classmates. You'll deal with these people for the rest of your life.

Welcome to professional school: It's all about networking.

Going forward, your classmates will refer clients to you, answer questions, serve as references, tip you off about jobs, and more. Don't screw them over for short-term gain.

Go out during fall of 1L year as much as you can. Get to know your classmates.

It's amazing how much socialization gets done (or missed) early on. 1L is when everyone meets everyone—the rest is just coasting.

There likely won't be all that many parties or group events as the term gets underway, but a weekly "bar review" outing is typical. When they happen, go.

Take a professor (or a teaching assistant, or a senior student) to lunch.

It's surprising how easy this is to do, and how few people actually do it. If a one-on-one seems forced, team up with a couple of classmates and take a different prof each week. And remember: There's plenty to talk about besides school.

Rankings & Grades

Hint: They matter. Here's how.

Your school's U.S. News ranking matters. A lot.

Like it or not, even when you're enrolled, your law school's ranking matters a great deal to you, your classmates, your future employers, and to the administration of your school. These rankings can (and often do) fluctuate, though once you've chosen a school, there's absolutely nothing you personally can do to affect them.

Your best defense against rankings obsession is to stay in the top 10% at a top 25 school.

There is an inverse correlation between your law school's ranking and the importance of your grades and extracurriculars.

Here's the rub: If you're at a top school and not shooting for the most prestigious clerkships or jobs, you can pretty much relax and do what interests you.

At a mid-level school, your grades matter both more and less than at a top 25 school: If you can't make the top 5-10% of your class, a Big Law job becomes dramatically less likely. In that case, aim to stay in the top half, and dedicate yourself to finding a job at a smaller firm. You can always lateral later on.

Your 1L grades may well shape your entire legal career.

On-campus interviews for 2L summer jobs are based on 1L grades—sometimes just the first semester.

Your first year performance can (and likely will) determine where you interview, which summer job you get, and consequently where you end up after graduation. This seems like a big deal, and it is.

Law school "senioritis" puts all others to shame.

Grades become progressively less important as law school goes on.

2L grades matter if you're in the handful of top schools where a judicial clerkship is an option, but even there, 3L grades serve no recognizable purpose for most students. Just stay above your future employer's grade thresholds.

Class Time

Keeping up with the day-to-day.

Everyone else is just as confused as you are.

When you start your first semester, rest assured that everyone else knows just as little as you. If it doesn't look that way, they're just better at hiding it. Seriously.

What you learn from class and what you need to know for the exam are practically mutually exclusive.

The case-based Socratic instruction often used in law school could just as easily be called "hiding the ball."

Don't get bogged down in facts and details: Almost every case boils down to one line of law. The sooner you learn to skim the case for that holding, the better. That's what will go into your outline, and that's what you'll need for the exam.

Keep the big picture in mind.

Context helps. Ask yourself how each new case fits into the overall landscape of the field.

The table of contents in your casebook provides a good overview. Make a one- or two-page, high-level outline for every class to keep the big picture front and center.

Stay current with class material.

Ideally, you'd read every assigned case in full and brief them all yourself.

In reality, doing this can be very time-consuming, particularly given the sheer quantity of assigned reading.

If you fall behind, catch up by looking up the cases in an outline or commercial guide. Keeping up to date is more important than going through the motions of reading and briefing every time.

Don't worry if you mess up in class.

Everyone does it and nobody cares, including the professor.

Just move on.

Find the note-taking system that works for you.

Don't worry about what everyone else is doing. There is no single best approach.

Careful textbook markup with six different color-coded highlighters might work for your classmate, but not for you.

Try different styles.

At least once, try taking class notes by hand.

You might like it. It's guaranteed to keep you engaged, listening, processing material, and off YouTube.

Turn off your wireless during class.

This requires more discipline than you might think, but it pays dividends. A good law school class discussion is not something you can (or should) follow between emails.

Remember: You're paying for this.

Start your legal writing assignments early.

Get something down on paper early on and develop it. Students who underperform in legal writing often start their papers far too late and don't have time to get their inevitable questions answered.

Exam Time

Law school exams are often worth 100% of your grade. Here's how to do them right.

Don't rely exclusively on generic commercial course outlines.

Commercial outlines make life easy by distilling core cases to their holdings and presenting them in predigested outline format.

These are useful aids. But the professor selected specific class material for a reason, and will often ask about it on the exam—whether or not it's in your commercial outline.

Check if your school (officially or not) has an outline bank.

You can either prepare your own outline by reading and briefing cases, or you can use an existing one from a classmate or student in a prior year's class. Some schools have outline banks organized by course and professor. Material may change somewhat from year to year, but these are great in a pinch—and far more tailored than a commercial outline.

EXAM TIME

When preparing for exams, work through real questions from real past exams under real exam conditions whenever possible.

Find out well in advance whether your law library keeps previous course exams on file. Whenever you can, use exams given by the same professor, since styles can differ dramatically.

Beware: Some libraries still keep only physical copies that can be checked out, often at inopportune times—so get your copies made early.

EXAM TIME

Remember to sleep and exercise.

These help you think clearly. An extra hour of sleep often beats an extra hour of reading. It works.

Only join a study group if you want to.

For some reason, study groups have become enmeshed in law school lore. If you didn't study with a group in college, don't feel compelled to do so in law school.

Attend study sections run by course teaching assistants.

Teaching assistants are usually the very students who got the top marks in a particular course in a prior year. They're valuable resources for course material, but even more so for institutional knowledge. And they may well have helped prepare the exam.

On a law school exam, always argue both sides.

There are entire books on this topic, but in brief: Law exams aren't about jumping to the "correct" answer. What's rewarded is spotting issues and then analyzing each one from all sides.

Scientists in particular sometimes have a hard time with this, because they're trained to ferret out a single best answer. Don't. You'll be shown several (sometimes outlandish) fact patterns. Spot the issues, and describe the various arguments on each side.

EXAM TIME

On a law school exam, use as many of the facts as possible.

Facts are there for a reason. If your torts exam mentions a dolphin in a pond, make sure that dolphin makes it into your answer.

If all else fails during a law school exam, use a bunch of key terms. You'll probably net some points.

If you really don't know what's being asked, write whatever you know, pepper it with whatever terms you remember, and try to make it fit. It's better than nothing, and might sail past a lazy grader. And next time, learn the material.

EXAM TIME

After an exam, resist the urge to "debrief" with classmates.

Wildly different answers can get equally high (or low) marks. Discussing your answers with colleagues will just make you second-guess your performance—often for no reason.

You probably didn't do as well (or as poorly) as you think.

It's a common anecdote: Every 1L student has at least one exam they were sure they failed but ended up acing. (And the reverse, too.) Do your best, and wait and see.

EXAM TIME

Now, sell your casebooks.

Wouldn't it be nice to have a bunch of cool-looking law books on your shelf? Take it from us: It's not. They're heavy, already outdated, and they're pretty much never useful again.

7

Choosing Courses

As law school progresses, you can choose more and more of your classes. These tips will help you do it right.

If you're fortunate enough to attend a top school where almost everything is an elective, do yourself a favor and take the "black letter" law classes anyway.

Federal Courts. Administrative Law. First Amendment. Business Organizations. Federal Tax. If you're worried about grade impact, you can always plan to take some of these courses during 3L, when it's too late for grades to matter anyway.

And for goodness' sake, even if your school tells you Property is not mandatory, it is. Take it. (Looking at you, Yale.)

If you're thinking of litigation, Civil Procedure is perhaps the single most important class you will take in your entire law school career.

Appreciate this, and learn it. While it may seem dry and distant during your first year, these rules will eventually govern how you try a case. You can't do anything in court without them.

If you're set on becoming a corporate lawyer, only a few courses will actually be relevant to your future practice.

These include Securities Regulation, Accounting (some schools offer accounting for lawyers), Mergers & Acquisitions, and some tax classes. Beyond that, seek out practicum courses that deal with actual corporate agreements. But, as with most practice areas, it's easy to enter corporate law without taking any specific classes at all.

Take a statutory or regulatory class.

Law schools tend to focus on case law. But a great deal of real-world law comes from statutes and regulations. Take at least one class that teaches statutory interpretation.

CHOOSING COURSES

Where possible, choose classes by professor as much as by subject matter.

Almost any subject can be interesting with the right teacher. You'll learn more from professors you enjoy.

Clinic work can be among the most useful and rewarding course credit in law school.

Clinics allow you to work directly with clients and do real legal work supervised by practicing attorneys. This is great experience.

But beware, clinics can easily become all-consuming. Manage these commitments carefully, especially during 1L (if your school even permits 1Ls to do clinic work).

And if you never do a clinic, don't sweat it: They're great, but by no means required for a successful practice.

Have your day in court.

Law schools often don't provide a lot of practical experience. Take a day off and watch some cases at your local courthouse. (If you work with a clinic, you might even find yourself arguing there.)

Take a class outside law school.

Most law schools are part of larger academic institutions, and law students can typically enroll in classes in other departments. Especially towards the end of your time at law school, why not study something you like and meet some new people?

It's an opportunity that won't likely return.

Aiming High

Running & gunning: The prestigious stuff.

At top schools, you don't need to be a box-checker.

Here's a special meta-tip. When reading the other tips in this section, remember: Students, particularly those at top law schools, often focus on checking every prestigious box they can (law review, running student organizations, publishing a note, getting a clerkship, and so on). Don't chase achievement for achievement's sake. You've made it, now do what you actually want to do.

If you're shooting for a clerkship or a competitive position, try to join law review.

At the very least, it won't hurt. Some schools select applicants for law review based entirely on grades; others use only a test of legal citation formatting; still others hold a write-on competition in spring.

Even if making law review isn't grade-dependent at your school, employers may still assume that it is.

Countless employers and judges still assume, by default, that students on law journal had the best grades. You can use this to your advantage.

If you don't make law review, do something else.

Schools often have several secondary journals, which may be walk-on or may pluck from applicants who didn't make the top-tier journal.

These largely provide a similar experience and suite of editorial opportunities (albeit with a little less prestige). You can also participate in moot court, mock trial, work as a research assistant for a professor, and so on.

Give some real thought early on to potential papers and articles you could write.

Keep an eye out for topics that interest you, and talk to professors and other students about these areas of law.

Chance favors the prepared law student. The earlier you have some potential topics in the back of your mind, the easier it'll be to spot useful concepts or material that otherwise might go unnoticed.

Yes, you can submit a note or an article.

Several of your classmates may end up placing notes or full legal articles, sometimes in surprisingly prestigious law journals. It's not always the brightest students who do this—just those who are confident others will want to read what they have to say. Don't sell yourself short: You can submit papers, too. (At some schools, students on law review are required to submit notes, from which the Notes Committee will select several to publish.)

The easiest way to get a comment or note published is to find a circuit split.

Smart judges have already worked up both sides of the issue, and it's pretty much contentious by default. You just need to pick a side and bring some new fuel to the fire.

Submit your class papers for school prize consideration.

Law schools often offer prizes in various fields. Typically, very few students actually submit papers.

Tweak your class papers if you like, but, in any case, submit them in an appropriate category. Bonus: In addition to surprisingly thin competition, sometimes these prizes come with some endowed prize money.

You'll never win if you don't apply.

It's better to have one deep relationship with a faculty member than several superficial ones.

For recommendation letters, what you'll really need is one professor (or maybe two) to say you're the best student they have—not ten to say you're pretty good.

Don't be afraid to approach law professors early on to ask about research opportunities—they're often more receptive (and less concerned about your total inexperience in their research area) than you might think.

Applications & Interviews

Almost from day one, law school is about your next job. Keep these tips in mind.

APPLICATIONS & INTERVIEWS

Mind your deadlines when applying for summer jobs, especially with government entities.

Think outside the on-campus interview box: The State Department, for instance, has recently allowed students to split their 2L summer with a law firm. But you need to apply early, so check with your career services office and keep track of deadlines.

Every year, countless people think of cool places to work only once the application deadline has passed. This is particularly true for 1L summer employment.

Before on-campus interviews, determine the main practice areas of the firms and offices you're interviewing with.

Firms aren't on campus to fight over the "best" student—they're there to fill a handful of summer spots in a given office. Even in Big Law, different offices can have distinct practice areas and specialties—so, if you declare your passion for a given field during an interview, make sure the particular office you're applying to actually handles that type of work.

You may be a generalist at this point, and that's fine, but don't take yourself out of the running by choosing a specialty that no one in the office actually does.

Think of some questions to ask your interviewers.

Typically, the interviewers conducting on-campus recruiting are attorneys. You're one of dozens of back-to-back interviews they're doing that day, and they're balancing this with their other work demands. They'll run out of things to ask you, and will ask whether you have any questions for them.

Have some.

If you're applying to firms or clerkships located far away from your school, be prepared to explain your interest in moving.

You may be surprised by how much interviewers focus on this. They're concerned that you'll come out for the summer but won't want to stay.

Good answers include actually having grown up in the area, having family there, or at least stating a desire to relocate there in the medium to long term. (This regionalism is less common when interviewing in major legal centers like New York and DC.)

Judges are people.

Don't select clerkships as if judges can be ranked like law schools, or even like law firms. Individual judges differ in ways that institutions do not. When interviewing, look for a good fit.

You don't necessarily need to line up a clerkship in 3L fall. Plenty of people ultimately land their clerkship several years out.

And as a bonus, due to idiosyncrasies in the government pay scale, those who clerk after several years of practice generally earn more, too.

10

Other Stuff

Some practical tips we picked up along the way.

Given a legitimate reason, some schools will arrange in advance to record lectures that you'll miss.

It pays to find out your school's policy on this ahead of time. No need to compound your stress when grandma gets sick.

Buy used textbooks where possible.

Some will have extensive highlighting and marginal notes. If you get a good one, these can actually be quite helpful.

If you're looking for an even cheaper option, forego the casebook entirely and print out the cases yourself from your legal research account. (Be aware, though, that casebook editors often trim cases down quite substantially.)

Don't worry about the bar exam just yet.

Law school is an unparalleled educational experience, and really interesting in its own right. So, don't sweat the bar exam just yet.

Enjoy school, do well, graduate, then take a major bar review class. Follow their program and they'll teach you enough to get through it—it's their whole business.

Study for the MPRE.

Take the Multistate Professional Responsibility Examination during law school. And don't be the one—and there will be one—who has to retake the test because you heard no one studies for it.

Money-saving tip: Major bar exam prep providers often hire class reps.

If you land one of these spots, your own bar prep class will likely be free. It also sets you up nicely to be a classroom attendant during the course, which ensures that you don't miss class, and nets you some money as well. Legal research providers typically hire reps, too.

OTHER STUFF

Westlaw and LexisNexis cost nothing to use and give away lots of free swag when you're a law student.

This goes way beyond a mini-mouse and a water bottle: Through shrewd use of Westlaw points, you can get an electric razor, a bicycle, or myriad other things from their catalog. This ends when law school does, at which point these services become punishingly expensive. Stock up.

Being a law student gives you entrée. Use it.

When you're an actively-enrolled student at a law school, you'd be amazed how many people will answer your e-mails, agree to be interviewed for a paper, or whatever.

Enjoy it: For whatever reason, this essentially stops dead when you graduate.

Concluding Words

Law school is a strange game, and when you're starting out, it seems like no one really knows the rules. It's crucial to hit the ground running, but how?

One way is to trust folks who've been there to distill what really matters and toss the rest. That's what we've tried to do here.

The truth is, there's no magic to doing well in law school, and good advice on how to do so shouldn't require a 300-page, prose-heavy manifesto. Our best tips, often quite simple, are all here.

We hope you've enjoyed *Law School Done Right*.

About the Authors

Michael Seringhaus is a 2010 graduate of Yale Law School, where he worked as a Coker teaching fellow and received the Burton H. Brody Prize in Constitutional Law, the Nathan Burkan Memorial Competition Prize in Copyright Law, and the Margaret Gruter Prize in Biology and the Law. He clerked for Justice Craig Stowers on the Alaska Supreme Court. He also has a Ph.D. in Molecular Biophysics and Biochemistry from Yale. He lives in Silicon Valley, where he practices biotech and pharmaceutical patent litigation.

Brian Savage is a 2010 graduate of the University of Michigan Law School, where he graduated *cum laude*. Prior to law school, he co-founded and managed three companies. He lives in Silicon Valley, where he practices corporate and securities law, representing a wide variety of technology companies, leading venture capital firms, public companies and underwriters in various corporate transactional matters.

Many thanks to our friends, colleagues, and classmates who contributed ideas, tips, and revisions. You did it right!

Made in the USA
Middletown, DE
12 August 2017